T0131635

Find You,
Fool You,
and Forget You

MATURE WOMAN

BALBOA.
PRESS

A DIVISION OF HAY HOUSE

Balboa Press books may be ordered through booksellers or by contacting:

Balboa Press
A Division of Hay House
1663 Liberty Drive
Bloomington, IN 47403
www.balboapress.com
1 (877) 407-4847

Print information available on the last page.

ISBN: 978-1-5043-3977-3 (sc)
ISBN: 978-1-5043-3979-7 (hc)
ISBN: 978-1-5043-3978-0 (e)

Library of Congress Control Number: 2015914202

Balboa Press rev. date: 09/09/2015

CONTENTS

Acknowledgments.. vii

Introduction ix

Chapter 1   The Power of Words 1

Chapter 2   Got Caught Up 7

Chapter 3   Life's Little Lesson...19

Chapter 4   All Genders Young and Old................................25

Chapter 5   What's Right and Wrong.....................................29

Chapter 6   Hold on a Little Longer.......................................35

Chapter 7   It Works Both Ways...43

Chapter 8   The Avenue "To Sex Crimes" 47

Chapter 9   What is Really Going on? 55

Chapter 10 I Have Feelings Too 63

Chapter 11 What's Your Level of Maturity? 73

Chapter 12 We Can Wait..77

Chapter 13 Shouldn't We Date First..79

Chapter 14 Learn from Each Other and Grow.......................85

Chapter 15 God's Way or Else 89

ACKNOWLEDGMENTS

I would like to thank God for allowing me to open my heart and life experiences with others in order to grow in love as they pursue their happiness. Special thanks to my daughter who inspired me when she was just a little girl, by asking so many questions about relations between men and women. And many thanks to my mom, for planting the seed of God in me when I was just a young girl. And of course, my husband for pushing me to go further, reminding me that there are no limits to how far I can go.

INTRODUCTION

I was inspired to write this book when my only daughter was a little girl. And we would ride down the street and see young ladies pushing their babies all alone. Very seldom do we see the baby's father's around. So I decided that I could hopefully give young ladies and men some insight on dating. Looking at my own relationships and others, I've seen some things over the years. Mainly that I was tired of putting myself in a position where I was being Found, Fooled, and Forgotten, as so many of us have. So basically this will help us to learn that a good foundation is necessary for a relationship to work. It must be built on solid ground, like a rock, not sand. To be able to make people see, both young and old the right way of pursuing a happy and healthy relationship. My main goal is to help people to see that dating followed by courtship, is supposed to lead to a happy marriage. When done God's way. To show what the difference is between the two and avoid all this heart ache, Lord knows I've had my share. I kept ending up miserable and never understood why. Until I really got into the word. You see most people have no idea how to select the right mate. They don't know the difference between dating and courting. Two things that simply must happen before marriage could even be considered. So I'm hoping to define both dating and courtship and the importance of them both. For example a date in simplest form, is merely a set time agreed upon by two people, to engage in an activity. And let's not forget courtship "a word practically forgotten". Most people know virtually nothing about the principles of courtship or it's true purpose. So this book is to enlighten us on the difference between the two. In hopes that we may allow God to take our hand and lead us to our right mate.

This book is to enlighten us on the difference between the two, that is dating and courtship. I want to emphasize that this book is meant for both genders and the goal is for them to learn how to better relate with each other. So that they can move forward in pursuing a more serious courtship, which can lead into marriage. Which is the real perspective of God's word. To be led down the right path ending in true happiness.

FIND YOU, FOOL YOU, AND FORGET YOU

The Power of Words

Keep Thy Heart with All Diligence for Out Of It Are the Issues of Life

Ever notice just how much words affect our lives, how one little word or phrase could catch your attention. Words may not always affect you immediately but they have a way of coming back and punching you right smack in the face. Words can make you have a whole different outlook on life especially when there said in the right way. You'll find yourself just sitting listening and pondering on what was said to you at this certain time. A lot of times it'll make you have a whole new outlook on yourself and boy can it be powerful at times, both emotional and spiritual. Sometimes it can be just what you need, a confirmation of what God had already placed in your spirit. Just like the word say he know us better than we know ourselves. Quite often we venture out in life thinking we know exactly which way were going, not knowing what we're going to run into. You see life has so many twists and turns you'll be faced with many choices. Only thing is we must make one whether we're right or wrong we must make a choice. Question is, how we handle the consequences from the choices we make? Will we choose to handle it on our own, our own understanding? Or will we turn to our father for answers, whom art in heaven, whom which we can do nothing without. Of course, let's be real, will be making most of these decisions on our own, you know what I mean, most of our lives we make our own choices, not consulting God for anything. Come on you know us humans we often think we know it all, especially, I'm sad to say, us women. Just like Eve we think we can break the rules and turn things around. Come on ladies, you know we have something inside us that tell us we can change the world, especially the male species. All yeah, we think we got what it takes to make the opposite sex turn into a man or whatever it is we want them to be. Ladies you know what I mean. A let's not leave out the fact that we are strong willed, especially when it comes to love.

Some stronger than others, but when we want what we want things can get a bit crazy. And no, I'm not leaving out the men, can't do that. They are more than likely out to get what they want from the beginning. Rules don't apply, when they have their eye on something or someone, talk about being persistent. Men can be very creative and in a lot of ways downright dirty, I mean no holes barred. Seems as though they know exactly what to say and what it is we want and need to hear. All yeah, they can be very persuasive when they want to. Let's face it, they love the chase. And a lot of ways you can say they are like a lion. They set their sights on the easy prey first, wear them down, get there fill and move on.

Always, mind you, thinking of their next victim, most of the time he had it lined up, already, working on it. You see this may take a little more planning. It is not as easy for this one as it was the first. As we all know over the years of growing up there were always the easy ones and the hard ones. But that just made it more interesting for the chase. This is why life is about choices, for all of us there are choices. See we're free to make our own choices God made sure of that, only thing is, most forget that there are also consequences. And one thing about it we can't choose those. We never know what they're going to be or when they are going to come. That's why it's best to think before you leap. You can't listen to everything you hear. Consequences can be very painful and not even what you expect. In fact you really don't know, but one thing about them they don't go away. They'll be waiting around the corner, and will come when you really don't expect them to. This is part of the journey, growing up. You see choices don't just start when you're grown up, they start early in life. But when our heavenly father breeths breath in our bodies the journey begin. And with that first breath so does our purpose. Oh yes, we have a purpose whether we realize it or forward and began to worship the Lord. Program first yourself and consciousness, praying that you turn yourself within and prepare yourself mentally, emotionally, and spiritually. Remembering many will find you, fool you, and forget you. It's all a part of the journey.

CHAPTER 2

Got Caught Up

Looking back at my experiences, I've had my share of heart aches and pain. Because of the choices I made. Talk about fine you, fool you, forget you, I fell head first. Yes he found me, made me feel like I was his queen, made me feel like I was the best in the world. Like no other could ever take my place, I mean I was all in. He could do no wrong, oh yeah he found me all right. Made me feel like I was number one, like I was all he needed, all yeah he found me. This man really went all out for me. He took me on shopping sprees, he wined and dined me for a few months, introduced me to his daughter, mother, and other family members. Made me think oh yeah this is it. I found myself changing. I began to put my all in this man totally forgetting what I wanted. I mean I really wrapped my everything into this relationship. I guess you could say I really had on my blinders at this point thinking only of the finish line, the wedding, It's okay to say I narrowed my sites too much and that goals are great as long as you remain open to better ones.

I was so into this man, that when the enemy came and blindsided me I didn't even notice. You see I thought he could do no wrong. We would run into his ex and she would say things like hey I need to talk to you one-on-one and at that time I would think nothing of it. I couldn't see what the enemy was doing, it just flew right over my head, now that I think of it he was cheating all along. And little did I know being so young he had been pulling the wool over my eyes for a while. You see everything my mother taught me had been put on the back burner. I was all in, I felt like I could handle this all on my own. Don't get me wrong my mother talked to me quite often. But you know how that goes when you're being led by the flesh and not the spirit. At the time it went in one ear and out the other. Most of us know when were young, we seem to know everything. Everybody else crazy but us. So my mother stepped off a little, decided to let me bump my head for a while, while she prayed me through. Don't get me wrong, she never left me. She monitored my life from behind, instead of having to fight with me. You see she knew what she had planted in me, the word. So anyway, being so captured by this man at the time I decided to commit myself to him. Meaning I would follow him anywhere. Mind you the word marriage never came into the picture. Oh, but I didn't care at the time I was in to deep. Even though I knew the right way, you see here come that word choice. That's just what I did, I made a choice. I followed him to St. Louis Missouri. You see he was working for GM and they transferred him there and of course he asked me to come live with him there, and no, the word marriage never came up. But yet I packed up most of my things, you notice I didn't say all my things, just some. I realize I wasn't ready to leave the nest. Like I thought, once again, that seed my mother planted in me started budding. Anyway, I made the choice to go ahead and go anyway, not thinking about those consequences waiting around that corner. Being faced with challenges and knowing what's right and wrong, because of my upbringing. I remember thinking to let go and let God. But the first step is to release, let go of what it is I'm holding to I remember thinking.

So here I am on my way to experience something new in my life definitely finding out what it is I'm holding to. Here I am with all my luggage on my way to the bus station not knowing I'll have to handle all this luggage by myself. You see the bus is not like the plane where they take care of your luggage for you, for a price. Oh, but I learned, boy did I. So I preceded on, I managed to get everything loaded and got comfortable in my seat ready for my trip, I didn't really think everything out, I was just ready to go and get to Norris the man who could do no wrong so I thought. So I proceeded on with my long long bus ride. I remember we got to a town and not knowing we had to do a transfer over to another bus. The driver announce this over the intercom and my heart sank. There was no one there to help me with all my luggage and I had so much, remember I was going to stay. So I struggled to get all my things off one bus and onto the other. I had to take a chance and leave my things and go back and forth to get everything onto the other bus. I thank God nothing happened to my things. I only wore myself out. I remember thinking why didn't he get me a plane ticket. Cheapskate. Well I made it through that ordeal, got comfortable in my seat and continued on my way.

So here I am a young lady in love for the first time ready to face whatever comes my way. Because I chose to take on this challenge knowing I should have gotten married first. But you know us women we think we can change anything, thinking marriage was on the way once I reached my destination. You couldn't tell me this man didn't love me, and I was ready for whatever came my way, not knowing it won't all be pretty.

Talk about fool you. The bus finally reached my destination, I looked around as I got off the bus thinking, I think they brought me to the wrong town! I mean this place was like a one buggy town in the middle of nowhere. So I gathered all my things from the bus and found myself standing there surrounded by luggage and no one in sight. Remind you, I'm just a young lady. I can remember thinking what have I gotten myself into? Choices. A few minutes passed and Norris rolled up, talk about happy. He loaded all my things into the car and off we went.

You see he hadn't been there very long his self so he was living in the comfort Inn which was a newly made hotel in Wentzville Missouri. He had not found an apartment yet. So we stayed there for a while. Just me and him one on one. Mind you the word marriage still had'nt come up. But I was in love so I had lots of patience. But we all know they run out. Norris would get up and go to work every day. He would come home and we'll go out and eat dinner. Come back clean ourselves up and lounge around. We did this for days and no, marriage never came up. I began to get bored with the program I wanted more. I wanted to work or go to school or something, but he will have nothing of the sort. So we end up moving to another town, a town called Normandy. This town was way better than the last. There were more people to converse with, I began to make friends and learn my way. You see we only had one car and of course he took that to work every day, so I had no way of getting around, just the way he wanted it. Never once did I ever lose sight that I have freedom of choice and the power to act on wise choices. I can turn around at any time. The choice is mine. Don't think I haven't searched my heart for directions trusting the right judgment and divine wisdom is still available to me. Now when I think about it he liked being in control, having me grounded. He may have liked it, but I hated it. Not only that you see I am a very outgoing person, a people person you might say. So you understand what I mean. But me being in love I continue to ride the ride a little while longer.

So we stayed in this town for quite a while that is until I started branching out more. I decided hey I need something to call my own like a paycheck. So I went out and got me a job learned the bus route so I would have transportation there and back. Talk about excited, I couldn't wait for him to get home and share the news with him. So he finally comes home a little late this day and I wait until we finish our dinner and everything before I break the news. So we were relaxing and I decided I'll tell him my great news. This was the day the devil stuck his head out. I proceeded to tell him that I have found me a job where I could take the bus back and forth. As I sat and waited for his reaction all I heard was silent. Then I finally got the reply that I had expected. Why would you go and do that he says? I make enough money for both of us. So I replied, I don't want all the strain on you, also I'm use to having a check that is made out to me, oh he'll have none of that he says. I remember him saying you don't have to worry about anything. I'm going to take care of you, All I can think about is when was the last time I went shopping other than the grocery store. You see I was a very independent woman and was use to getting what I want, I mean it's not like we were married. You see I was a young lady not too long graduated from school so I had dreams and ambitions and drive I was not ready to be bound to staying in the house cooking and cleaning, Just for the short-lived thrill. I was ready to start making my dreams come true, and was ready to do it with him, since he already had a good job I thought maybe I could go to school and work. Believe me I was not one of those women who thought that she should depend on a man taking care of her. You see all of this was briefly discussed before we even made this move, but you know how that goes and no, the word marriage still hadn't, come up. You know what they say they change when they get away from home.

So a few more weeks went on, and I still was playing house. I never got that job because he didn't want me to. So here we go up and moving to another town. This time into an apartment I was excited this time no more hotels. Thinking things would be changing since we were a little more settled. Okay, now I can really find me a job, start going places really getting to see St. Louis. Instead of him going to work and I stay home. No I was tired of living like this remember I was a very young lady, he was older than me, but what that supposed to mean. I was ready to live a little. Do something. And he loved life as much as I did. Don't get me wrong I was aware that he worked hard every day, so I didn't press him too much. But I began to notice that he started coming home later and later, at first it didn't bother me because I had met me some girlfriends who's men were working at the plant like mine. So I had some company now. I started filling alive again. Being so outgoing and jovial as I am.

I have endless possibilities that are available to me. I am not limited to any one path. The best is yet to come. While the guys were at work me and the girls would get together and play cards talk, do each other hair, we would even read the Bible together. This really helped me through the day even though I had finally got some company, I couldn't stop thinking of my own dreams and wants. I still wanted to go to school and work more than ever. As time went on I began to learn my way around because there was only one car, and yes it was his Norris start coming home later and later which made me very uncomfortable. I wanted to know why all of a sudden this was happening. It wasn't like this before, and my mother didn't raise no fool. I started meeting more and more people both male and female. I guess that's sort of threw my focus off the fact that he was staying out longer and longer. Remember they do believe you. So one particular night my girls were over, we were doing what we do waiting for our men to get home. Everybody's man made it home but mine. I kept my cool, I didn't allow myself to get excited because the fact remains this is a choice I made. Remember, I said I was ready to take on anything that came my way. And of course, I can't choose my consequence.

I kept my head about the situation as time continued to pass. I was up all night thinking all kind of things not knowing which way to turn, remember I was down there all by myself. So I dealt with it the best way I knew. I got on my knees and began to pray. You see my awareness of God is the most fulfilling, for of all just knowing that I am eternally loved, I choose to soothe myself in body, mind and soul. I know that I have God's love and he's here for me. I asked the Lord to show me if this man was all right or is he just out being no good. I began to dry my eyes and started calling out to God, guide my steps Lord because remember greater in me than he that is in the world. I already knew that the choice I made was of the flash not of the Spirit. Talk about fool you. I started to feel as though I fooled myself, which I know I did when I chose to live this way. So like I said time had passed, in fact daylight had come and no Norris insight. So, what am I to do? Shall I blow up? Go off into a rage? Or should I kill him with kindness? You know,

I've been nothing but faithful and good to him from the beginning if he know like I knew, he would not mess with me. Get me miles from home and now you want to act a fool, not tonight. Tonight may be filled with new adventures but I feel a deep calm within, my journey through this night is in the spirit of peace. Peace is within me. At times unaffected by what's going on between me and this world. Remembering peace is God given and always within my reach. So I decided to reach out for the Lord

Well the party ended and of course, Noris was intoxicated. We got in the van riding with a friend of his whom was very nice I might add. So we're riding along and he started in on me, I guess since I've been putting up with him and his other mess he really began to think I was a pushover, wrong girl, as I often warned him. So he kept on pushing and pushing telling me I'm not going to work. Unless he allow me to. I mean he just kept at it until he felt like he had an S on his chest and he was drunk mind you, I was still sober in every way. He started filling a little frog-ish he leaped right over on me. Before I knew it I was on that man taking all my anger out on him. Thank God no one was hurt, but the next day you bets believe he knew he was in a fight. He licked his wounds and stayed in bed all day long. Next day he acted as if nothing happened. Talk about fool, you, I never thought our relationship would result to this, talk about change. Days went on. He continued to go to work come home late and even stay out every once in a while. But this is what broke the Campbell's back. One day we're at home with some company just chilling and haveing a nice time. All of a sudden there was a knock at the door, so I answered and there stood a short nice-looking woman. So I say yes.

You know I try to greet all people with friendly hospitality. Hospitality is one of my gifts. And as I give, I truly love to receive.

As an expression of the love of God in me, I welcome people into my home, she was no exception. So I asked what may I ask you want with him? She stood there looking stupid, and what comes out of her mouth is, Norse, can you take me to get some weed? Looking right through me mind you. I turned and looked at him, turned back to her and said, go get your weed how you been getting it and slammed the door right in her face. Then I proceeded to him, ask what in the world do you think you're doing? I told him the devil is a lie and I would not stand for this, nor will I fight with him. Talk about forget you. I asked him what was going on with her? And just as I suspected he had been cheating all along. I told him not only did he have no respect for me, and there definitely could be no love. I let him know you don't hurt nothing you love and that this relationship was over. I said that I wanted to go back home. He told me that he don't know how I'm going to get there because he don't want me to go. I thought he had lost his mind. Talk about forget you. You see I guess he thought I was his built in maid amongst other things. And this man really thought I was going to stay after all that's happened. He refused to give me a ticket home and I didn't want to call home crying for help. So I stayed a couple weeks more until I could come up with a plan. Remember I was young and dumb, but not to the point I would be used. Only dumb for making this choice.

Remember he was the breadwinner at the time, so I had to wait for him to get my ticket home. So I played it cool for a minute until he decided to stay out all night again. Talk about forget you. Yes he had got down there and totally forgot about me. Me, the one who was there when he had nothing going on. I sat there, waiting for him to come home, he never did. So I decided I'm not taking this anymore I'm going. My spirit is my compass on each step of this journey. I trust my intuition to guide me around stumbling blocks. And to give me new direction if needed. So I got up packed a suitcase and just started out the door, at night mind you. So upset I wasn't thinking of the demons that lurk at night. My faith is strong always have been, it was the grace of God that nothing happened to me that night. Here I am out here hitchhiking in Missouri, where there is mostly land. I'm trying to make it to the freeway. First I had to hitchhike a ride with a man whom I never seen a day in my life to get to the freeway and I thank God to this day he was'nt some kind of serial killer. Just because I was letting anger and pain lead me, "the flesh". So glory be to God, I made it to the freeway and he let me out no questions asked. I got on the freeway facing my way home. But, as I stood there with my thumb out, I remember thinking what am I doing out here on this freeway, cars flying past bright lights everywhere. All I can think is I don't have to put up with this, I'm going home. I realize while I was out there. That sinful pride. Pride is a sin and I thank God for sending an angel out there to get me off that freeway. Traffic was really moving, and all of a sudden a car pulled over, a man got out and approached me. I could feel nothing but goodness coming from him. I can truly say I was totally grateful to God for sending this man to help me in my time of need. Given thanks to move beyond doubt or worry, into a place of trust full of faith "I THESS" give thanks in all circumstances; for this is the will of God in Christ Jesus for you.

He asked me what am I doing out here with a suitcase? He asked me if I would please for my safety, get in the car so he can take me back to the apartment, I agreed and got into the car, I felt nothing but relief and blessed that he cared. He called my mom for me and told her the situation, and that he was taking her baby

CHAPTER 3

Life's Little Lesson

Yes this is what you would call a choice. A choice in my life that truly open my eyes to a broad of things. You see I wanted my will to be done. Forgetting what the right way should have been, marriage first. I chose to go for it and learned a valuable lesson in life. God's way is always right, for you can do nothing without him.

As I continue to live and experience this journey, and watch others go through. I've learned the Bible to be the inspired and only infallible written word of God. You see I was raised knowing the word, and I knew right from wrong. But no one ever said it would be easy, that they'll be no trials and tribulation. See everything is not black and white the important thing is to learn and become wise from your choices. No one can judge you but God. Don't beat yourself up. And

Of course this is not my only mistake in life I've made plenty.

And as I walk, and watch through this journey, I realize all the rules were already there, all the time, in the great book, the Bible. I had to learn and so will you, when all else fail try reading it.

I can remember riding down the street with my daughter when she was just a little girl, and we would have such great conversations. So one day as we were riding we noticed a young lady pushing a baby carriage. So we kept riding and there was another. So we glanced at each other with a slight smile. We continued on riding listening to our music, then we saw two more young ladies pushing their babies. My daughter turned and looked at me and said mommy why don't any of those babies have their daddies walking with them? All I can do at that moment is look at her and gasp for air. Make sure that I find the right words to say. I mean come on she's only eight years old I didn't want to confuse her or lie to her or just give my own opinion.

So this is what I told my daughter. Just what I had come to an conclusion of. When it comes to babies having babies, is, that boys are like bumblebees, they jump from flower to flower. And yes girls are the flowers. Bees like to pollinate the flowers, and that's what boys like to do to some girls. It's just their nature. My daughter looked and said, mommy why do you say that? And my answer to her was, because, boys at a certain age seem to be focused on one thing and one thing only. And that would be to pollinate the flowers (girls). Don't get me wrong, boys have other interests as well. But we seem to be their main interests. Boys are funny, cute and some awkward. But they are still like bumble bees. They can be sweet and kind. And they can be mean and nasty. Thinking about it, girls were quite unique as well, some more than others. We had our way of getting the boys attention as well. I'm talking fat girls, skinny girls, tall girls, short girls, black, white, yellow, whatever. We are plentiful. Just like flowers. And we don't hesitate getting what we want as well, we can be just as aggressive at times when we want to. I may have gotten a little long-winded with her, but we had quite a ways to go. So I continued talking.

I told her that times has changed since I was a little girl growing up. I tried to explain that when we were young there was a mother and father in most homes. How we had more freedom than the kids now, because there was always supervision somewhere around. We always had some type of activity going on. There was never a day that we had nothing to do. I think we were to busy and scared to think about sex. We didn't have two run out and buy everything they sold in stores, we were the make do people.

Part of the fun was making what we could not afford. Things like swing sets (a tree with a tire and rope), jump rope (a clothes line rope), Go carts (some wood and wheels off of a baby carriage), and let's not forget making your own bike with other bike parts, hopscotch, box hockey, for squares, basketball, marbles, and many other great ideas we could come up with. Yeah you could say I went way back there I got a little excited. My brothers were very inventive, they came up with all kind of ideas, so there weren't many dull moments at our house. Not to mention my brother's crazy friends we had our own little world everybody love to come over our house. Our house stayed busy, all our friends called my mother Auntie. I can remember the water fights during the summer. I remember one in particular, where we wet up anybody who came past the house. The whole town knew our house. This one day we decided to wet up anybody. So my brother decided to put the pool in the front yard and filled it up with water. He and his friends will pick people up by their legs and arms and throw them in the pool. I can only thank God no one got hurt or mad, it was all in fun. Plus it was a scorcher that day.

I'm saying this just to give you an idea of how loving people were back then. You didn't have to worry as much back then as you do now. Back then girls were ashamed to get pregnant out of wedlock. It was disgraceful to them and their family. Don't get me wrong there were heartbreaks back then too. I'm only trying to point out how much times have changed. Notice how the respect for life has decreased in people. How there is no respect for God, you, or anything else, which is why prayer is more important than ever nowadays. Without him we can do nothing, so I say to my daughter and others think before you leap.

Now I know these young ladies didn't choose to just go out and get pregnant nor did they plan to be raising a baby by their self. They were definitely caught by one of the bumblebees (the boy). They were found, pursued, and persuaded. Never in 1 million years did they think this would be happening to them because you see it take two to tangle a boy will persue you until he wear you down. Meaning all his focus is on the flower (the girl) at the time. Remember too much pressure will burst a pipe. Not to mention, all the competition. Girls can be very pushy to, especially if a guy they like is all into you. You see you may be one of those girls who was well raised and didn't care how much the boy said he like you. You knew to keep the skirt down and the panties up. Whereas this is a turn off for the boy but oh well. Sometimes it'll make him want you more or he'll start looking at the other girl who is ready, willing, and able. Don't mean he'll stop chasing behind you. He's going to play both ends if he can. He may not get to pollinate you, but he is definitely all over the other girl. He's already got things moving with her, and still have you on his mind. All yeah he most definitely found a live one. One whose willing, to do what you wouldn't do. And yes it happened more than once, so much, along came a baby, a baby he had no attention of taking care of. He really fooled her into thinking that he gave a darn about what happened to her. And yes she became one of those baby carriage pushers, ending up all by herself. After all this had happened you can bet he left her alone and continued pursuing the young lady he couldn't have. He totally forgot about her and the baby, because he got what he wanted and was ready to move on to the next flower. So now when we ride down the street and my daughter see a boy all hugged up on a girl, she would say to me, mama she is just a flower and he is just trying to pollinate her. And all I can say is Lord let these words stick in her heart.

CHAPTER 4

All Genders Young and Old

I'm not trying to make this book just focus on the young people. It is also for the older people as well. Just because we are a little older doesn't mean we don't get hurt too. Because every adult don't grow up or mature with their age. While everyone wants to be happy and assumes that following the crowd is the right way to achieve happiness, most remain miserable and never even know why. Most people just don't have no idea how to select the right mate. See dating, followed by courtship (a word many rarely use nowadays) is supposed to lead to a happy marriage, but marriage cannot be happy if it is not built on the right foundation, which begins long before the wedding day.

Some men and women have long relationships. They have kids one, two, or three or more, from which they build their relationship on. Now we all know that this method hardly ever end up right, because it is not what God intended. They usually end up never getting married, mostly by choice. And that's just sad when you look at it. Because no one wins and some are together for years. The couple loose, as well as the kids, most definitely the kids. All the time and energy gone to waste because they grow tired or part from each other, which simply means there was no real love between them. They left out dating and courtship and went straight to playing house.

Of course, the woman end up having to pull all the weight. Where she usually end up raising the kids on her own because the man usually moves on. Most of the time he starts a new family. And once again someone has been found, fooled, and for gotten, mainly because they chose their way and not God's way. Now I know things don't always go like that, but the majority of the time it do. There are times when the man gets the weight. He end up with his kids and get to experience the whole growing up of the kids and the woman is long gone doing her thing. Ever think that if we wouldn't call ourselves testing the waters first and do things God's way in the first place that maybe, just maybe things would turn out right more often, if we could just stop trying to do everything our way and give God's way a try we could avoid a lot of this pain. Just taste and see what God can do. I'll tell you as long as you keep him in it, you won't go wrong that's for sure. All yeah, I just said something there because I took that advice and used it in my own life. And God for me took evil and turned it too good. I was a single parent looking for love in all the wrong places, but God kept me and he didn't let go. If it had not been for his grace and mercy where would I be, I often ask myself. You see here we go back to those choices. And, there consequences. Which can be avoided, if we make better choices. Many simply do not understand that premarital sex is harmful and is sin, and ruining otherwise potentially healthy relationships.

I do remember when I was young watching different couples go through their ups and downs. I remember a young lady getting pregnant by this guy who she really cared for so she thought. Yeah, I remember how he found her at this party we had went to and she really fell for him. I mean he was one of the star basketball players at our school, and he was a very nice-looking guy. As time went on they continued to see each other for quite a while. He really had his hooks in her, she was truly smitten. One night we had a school dance everyone was there. And, in come Mr. Man with another girl just smiling, head all up in the air. You know this had to affect her and of course it did. So she took it upon herself to approach him, and he totally ignored her as if she didn't exist, talk about find you. I guess he thought it was a joke. Oh, he really found and fooled her. But you know that's those bees for you she was just another flower which got pollinated by someone who was'nt worth her time. I mean the girl was crushed, but she came through with the help of her friends. Only thing is she got pregnant by this pig. And of course he really acted a complete idiot. He not only treated her as if she'd never exist, he totally denied the baby. I would never forget the anger I developed for this man for treating this girl in such a way. He totally forgot her. He wanted nothing else to do with her or the baby. I truly wanted to do bodily harm to him, but, like I've said before there are consequences for our actions. And being a strong young lady with a good head on her shoulders she was able to get through this with God's forgiveness and grace. You see she realized that it was just as much her fought as well, because she chose to give her self to this idiot. She see, now that God's way is always the right way. He may have forgot her, the guy that is, but

God never will. Nor will he ever forsake you. This is why she turned out to be just fine, the second time she learned from her mistake. She was married before she had her second child and chose to make better choices.

CHAPTER 5

What's Right and Wrong

I realize that each experienced in my life has given me the strength, courage, and power to make the necessary change I need in my life, whether physical or spiritual. If I am on a path that is unhealthy for me, I began to inner search knowing I can turn around at any time and choose a new path. It's never too late to turn your life around. Just know you have freedom of choice and the power to act on wise choices where you can expect, a better outcome. A more tolerable consequence. Go ahead and look for ways to start a new, to God be the glory for new beginnings, un restricted freedom. And there is definitely nothing wrong with that. We all take risk each and every day. I use to hesitate or hold back when faced with some of life's new opportunities. Scared of failure, or what others may say. I grew out of that quick. Especially with God on my side. Now I move forward with confidence. Knowing that with God on my side I'm a winner at all times even when things don't go the way I think they should. Stepping out of my comfort zone, the less certain about the outcome. Not allowing myself to be vulnerable or to become the prey. Letting others take me for granted. You see as a woman I've learned that a man will play you as close as you allow them to. You either sink or swim.

I'm thankful for many things in my life. And one of the main things is being able to determine that my relationships were based on the wrong foundation I'm thankful to be able to have a decern spirit as I mature. You see Satan comes to kill, steel, and destroy. Not to mention his deceitful ways everyone understand a fake or forge, his main goal is to create a counterfeit that is totally and distinguishable from the original. So with this being said, consider, counterfeit Christianity. You would not offer a statue. You would offer something that look, feels and seem to be Christianity in order for it to appear real, that's what the devil does. Now let's closely examine one of the biggest breakouts produced by the greatest forges of all time, true love. The Bible has described three forms of real true love. The devil has produced counterfeits to these, which among other things form a faulty foundation for dating today. Many misconceptions and definitions about love abound. Some feel that is devotion, others feel that it is sexual passion, and of course there are those who feel it is affection. Then we have those who feel it is adoration, or respect, caring, admiration, and oh yes let's not forget warm feelings. Some even see it as a mystery that can't be solved. So they asked what love is? It is evident that a lot of us simply do not understand true love. Problem is so many initially felt that a relationship was right, when it was not. So many think that they are in love only to find out that their feelings were little more than "easy come, easy go". Most people value their relationship on the opinions of their panel of experts, their friends, who most of the time don't even have a significant other theirself, but is quick to give their opinion. But how can that be? When they don't know the true meaning of love.

There are many different kinds of different love, romantic, parental, platonic. Mostly love is filling emotionally attached to another person. We want to be close to that person. We want understanding. We want sharing. We want to care and have someone care for us. Let's face it romantic love usually comes with a strong physical or sexual action. We want to hold, touch and sometimes become sexual with that person. Lust is a physical attraction, which can sometimes turn into love. Other people get together and they have a really strong physical connection. When two people fall in love, lust usually fade away and is replaced with a deeper more intimate emotional connection. It's usually hard to tell the difference between the two. Usually time tells. Let's face it everyone wants to be close, to share, to understand and to care for another person. This idea of love is a classic mixture of good and evil. Remember Adam and Eve chose the knowledge of good and evil. We must realize that Satan's goal is to make his counterfeit seem right – feel right – seem and feel natural. However, close scrutiny will expose the counterfeit, the common misconception and lead you to understand true love, many speak of true love. Virtually all people would say that they are seeking this. Question is, is it love or what we call infatuation? Sad to say so many spend their entire life looking for true love, but never finding it. Truth of the matter is that most don't understand the difference. With this being said, remember that what seems right can lead to disaster (Proverbs 14:12 16:25) it requires honest examination to determine the difference between true love and infatuation. The definition of infatuation come from the French word "fatus" meaning fool – or foolishness. Webster's define it as: to make foolish; to act with folly; to weaken the intellectual power of; or to deprive of sound judgment. So therefore, in one sense people have become infatuated could be considered fools, so of course, few would admit the choices they've made are foolish. And most would never admit their foolish. Actually, because they are caught up in the feelings of infatuation which usually start with a crush. Infatuation can involve a very powerful attraction, never underestimate it. For it can stir up emotions and feelings that can make you think you are in love. When it is nothing more than a romantic daydream, that make you feel as if you're going through a wonderful experience that will last forever. Infatuation happens quickly whereas love always develop much slower. Anything of worth takes time.

With love, one's interest becomes deeper and more consistent with time. Infatuation on the other hand involves feelings, hot lust to the extreme, while love involves patients, balance and temperance. Truth is one cannot fall in love at first sight. Real love is not something that happens by chance. It develops over time, based on the all important foundation that the creator has given us. People do not fall in love but rather they fall in lust. Only thing is, lust has purely selfish motives, and concerned only with fulfilling its own desires and wants. That can turn into love eventually, but not with advice from society, such as planned parenthood which places little emphasis on abstinence or self-control, but only on being careful when sexually active. This only serves to fuel this selfish desire, called the lust John was inspired by Christ to write: for all that is in the world, the lust of the flesh, and the lust of the eyes, and the pride of life, is not of the father, but is of the world. (I John 2:16). This is how John divides all that is in the world into these three categories; lust of the flesh, lust of the eye and pride of life, the basic sex drive, one of the most powerful forces behind dating today. People practice sizing up each other for sex every day. For years "girl watching and boy watching has been a national pastime millions often lust after men and women to whom they are not married to". While God did instill the sexual desire in human beings for pure and holy purpose, the world is held by Satan's influence of lust. So just stop and think for a moment the way the world typically date, court and consequently get married. Basically, today God's commands are often broken. Throughout society people are confronted with temptation to lust, adultery, fornication and many other things. Almighty God created sex. It is one of the most wonderful physical experiences that man and woman can share. Yet Satan has twisted this God design pleasure. Reducing it to a sinful act, practice almost nationwide between virtual strangers. You see sex has pre-occupied the minds of our young so that in time it destroys their character and ruins any potential for a happy, wholesome, lifelong relationship between a husband and wife. You see what John meant by "lust of the eye". Not to be considered hot and sexy lust is deeply enriched with a human nature. Many discard their virginity after a night of clubbing merely because someone seemed sexy. Talk about fine you, fool you, forget you. Understand! Those who seek to please God are not to fulfill the lust of the flesh. Yet millions do this exact thing when dating and do it almost nonstop. Many don't use common sense. But rather follow their hormones into wrong relationships.

Lust is the fuel for sex and vice versa. Many simply do not understand that premarital sex is harmful and is sin running otherwise a potential healthy relationship. The flesh manifests

CHAPTER 6

Hold on a Little Longer

Dating today has not changed much from years ago. We all can stand to learn more about dating and courting. Learn that this is not something you just pick up from others, because more than likely they don't know. It's just a hard cold fact that today's standards of dating and courting are wrong, all wrong. There is no testing the water. You can avoid being found, fooled and forgotten.

There are numerous forms of dating today much more than years ago. Yet singles and teens are left with no choice but to accept what is offered for those looking for love.

I can remember back in the day clubbing was the thing. Perhaps one common setting for meeting people, this mostly involved trying to find dates, or more often one night stands. In an atmosphere of loud music, drugs and alcohol. A breeding ground for the bumblebees (men), looking for loose women who are intoxicated and filling sexy and ready to be pollinated or whatever may come their way. Don't get it twisted because the men are being preyed upon as well.) Like at prayer mantis. they are all in position to be found, fooled and forgotten. This atmosphere, and these places, cause participants to lose all self-control. Men find it easy to grope and fondle women bodies at any time while dancing. And if you see the way they dance nowadays, you would say it is nothing less than an orgy set to music. Plus the music is so loud that conversations are practically impossible. Now tell me could anyone in such an environment, filled with alcohol and focused on the thrill of the moment, possibly employ sound reason and logic to make right dating choices? The clear answer is no! Rather they focus only on fulfilling sexual urges and desires! It merely revolves solely around selfish lust and instant gratification.

Most are definitely looking to be found. Like I said before, men aren't the only one's who like to chase and watch, this is a known fact for both genders.

A story comes to mind of how a young lady I know who came across her first heartbreak. She was involved with a DJ, he was her first love. He blew up and felt that he should spare her from all the heartache which would have been coming her way at least that was his story. All it really was, was just another case of find you, fool you and forget you. All he really did was made her heart hard. Not realizing that they had made a soul tie. He was her first. This was the man she chose to give her virginity to. So of course, this breakup had to be devastating for her. Just another reason to keep dating and courtship, God's way. Leaving out fornication, keep abstinence first. It's much less painful for the heart. Anyway, time went on she eventually got over it. But the flesh

Had began to take over. She decided to go to the club with her sister and some friends one night, you know, just to get out and mingle. Not realizing she was hungry, hungry for companionship. Because she knew what it felt like, and of course, she knew she had what it took to get the attention she was longing for. And you best believe Satan was going to make sure this was easy for her to achieve. So, as she sat at the table with her sister and friends, amongst people she's really not accustomed to. Being led by the flesh mind you, everyone started ordering their drinks which truly amazed her, because they ordered drinks that were on fire. That alone was something she had never experienced. Let alone going to a nightclub to meet someone, in hopes he'll be the one to ease her pain. As I mentioned before Satan* deceives the whole world" (Rev. 12; 9). That's right you heard me correct the whole world. It is in the Bible. Remember now, Ms. girl had a taste of lust. So she wasn't thinking straight in the first place. Remember the word, he seek home he may devour (SATAN). Okay here is a 20 year old young lady whom is really new to all this, except for the fact that she was dating a DJ. But, yet she has chosen her own path. Setting aside what her mother had bestowed in her. Going in with eyes wide open, and an agenda on her mind. Ready to mix it up. A mixture of good and evil. Ready to take another ride on that roller coaster of extreme. Ready to experience something new. Looking for love once again.

So as she sat and time moved on, and she started weighing her options of men in the club. She noticed one guy, one guy who caught her attention. So she started asking the girls at the table about the guy. And Lord and behold of course, her sister knew this guy. She began to tell her what it is she knew about him. Which wasn't very much. So after all that guessing, her sister went over and got him, to introduce them. But, as he was on his way over from across the room, all she could say to herself is wow! yummy! He had a body second to none. And of course, the works of the flesh are manifest. Her heart started to flutter. Palms of her hands became wet, eyes bulging, and mind racing thinking what am I going to say? Say to this magnificent looking man, who was approaching fast. And boom, he's here in my space, and I'm loving every minute. Here I am sitting here knowing I'm very vunerable, not thinking clear. Just hurt, and wanting to be loved, held, touched or caressed, something I have become accustomed to from my previous relationship with Dre. I wanted to defeat loneliness. I found myself in a situation more intense than I expected. Not only did I find him attractive, the feeling was obviously mutual this man came at me full speed ahead. I mean you could feel the lust in the air coming from the both of us. If seem as if he was feeling the same way I was. He pursued me in such a way I found myself gasping for air. I mean come on, I was looking hot that night, and out for the hunt. But I never expected it to be so dramatic. Still to this day I can remember the way we said our names to each other. I'm talking it was hot. Next thing I know this man was all up on me. Touching softly, rubbing my back as he spoke. Next thing I know were kissing. Tongue all down my throat, we were kissing with passion. At this point everything I knew to be right didn't matter. My flesh had took control. I was allowing this man to touch me in places I know he had no right. But I was all in, not only had I found what I was looking for that night, I was found as well.

Now you would think, that I will want to take it real slow, being that I was filling wounded from my past relationship. That may be so, but I was ready to get back into the dating world. So I thought. Even though things didn't turn out the first time I was still willing to try. I wanted love and a happy marriage as well as any other women. Though I must admit the way things are set up, society leaves us minimal places from which to draw potential mates. So therefore, it is of the utmost importance that every precaution is taken. I know this to be true. But come on, when the flesh take over the situation is hard to think clear, which is what happened in my case.

Don't get it twisted I'm not an easy girl, but this filling felt so right that I just knew it couldn't be wrong. So as the night came to an end I proceeded out the club to my car. He was fast on my trail. He kept at me, all the way to the car. He began to beg and plead for me to go home with him. This went on for at least an hour or more. Kissing and hugging me with such a need of my company. Things were moving a little too fast for me. I started having all kind of thoughts. I didn't want this mixture to be fatal. Nor did I want to be just another notch on his belt. So I stood my ground, not allowing my flesh to lead me into thinking that sex is good in practically any situation. I'm glad I was able to regroup. Because this man had his hooks in me already. We went ahead and pulled ourselves together, exchanged numbers and went on our way. Time will tell if this was just a hot crush or something that could turn out to be the real thing. I am just glad I did'nt allow it to be a one night stand.

> The next morning I woke up with butterflies in my stomach and this man on my mind, on my mind all the day long. I'm happy to say that the feelings were mutual. He called me bright and early the next day. Which brought my heart joy he called me all day while at work and even more when he got home. We talked for hours. Then he finally got me to come

over. I thought in my mind I would be strong enough to handle him. Especially since we were not at the club or anything, we both were well rested and had our heads altogether. Boy, did I fool myself. Before I could even get in the house good, I found my clothes coming off. All yeah we, really found each other. Things got so hot between us. I found myself in his bed before I knew it. The both of us confessing our love for each other, Yep just like that.

We were so in lust with each other we skipped dating and Courtney. We were with each other daily. You couldn't have told me that this man and I would not be getting married. Yes that's right married. Our feelings were just that strong, at least I thought, remember I chose my own path this time.

As time went on we started planning a baby. Yes, a baby. I'm telling you, the hooks were deep in me. I didn't have any kids nor did he. So I decided to stop taken my birth control, due to the fact it was time for it to come out anyway. I went to the Dr. and got my implant taken out so I can become fertile again. This was a decision we both made.

Knowing I knew the correct procedure about a man and woman having a baby. I knew I should have been married first, and that God's way is the right way. But we all make choices that we are willing to take the consequences for sometimes, and you can say that I was one of those people.

We made our choice together, and within the next month I

was pregnant. We were both filled with joy, and little did I know he would propose to me. I must admit it made me feel better even though I just wasn't ready. I didn't think it would be right for us to marry after the fact. I know that what had happened between us was not of God, even though we really did love each other. As time went on, I found myself backing off because I started to feel that I allowed myself to be played. I say this, because after I turned him down in marriage he started back seeing other people. So the love I thought we had must not have been real like I thought. Even though we were still seeing each other. We never till this day stopped loving each other, I feel as though I fooled my own self in so many ways. But I am grateful for our love child. Even though we're not actually a couple today, we still refuse to give anyone else our all because of the soul tie we have.

CHAPTER 7

It Works Both Ways

Just another reminder of how old Satan work; remember Adam and Eve in the Garden and how the devil tried to discredit God, and appeal to their vanity. There were two special trees in the garden, first the tree of life representing God's way. They could eat from this tree as they wished. Then there was that tree of the knowledge of good and evil, which they were forbidden to eat from. God told them that in the day that they do eat from this tree they would surely die, you see they had a clear choice, just like them, we have a choice this is one of the main reasons we find ourselves getting used and abused. Because of the path we choose to take. Most seem to like the short-lived thrill of being used and tossed aside, going on to the next, searching and searching for someone to love them. And most never finding it because they chose their way never God's.

It's safe to say when they chose the forbidden fruit (Adam and Eve) they handed us to the serpent's way of thinking. Especially when it comes to dating, courtship, and marriage. That is why it is so important we take time to see what's at stake. Knowing that marriage is right next to salvation. Knowing the importance of laying a right foundation for loving your mate and your mate loving you. Avoid being found, fooled, and forgotten. Haven't you heard, love is a two-way street. Most of us live our lives guided by feelings some by a mere momentary impulse. Not really seeing what lies ahead, pure heart ache, if it's not of God.

Think if you will, about the beginning of a relationship, you know when you're having a good time, everything seems wonderful. As if you're floating on air. Then all of a sudden old Satan throws a curveball into the scenario. What you thought was the beginning of something great, he put a stop to it.

By simply getting in our mind. Most people live their entire lives completely unaware of why things "start right" or "go wrong". What they are unable to do is grasp that what they do or do not do, has a direct effect on their lives. We must recognize that for every cause there is an effect, and for every effect there is a cause. And that this is a law. Not only is this in physics, the same is true in life.

Take a hard look, if you will, at the world around you. You'll notice that many are familiar with the many formulas of "falling in love". But the truth is that one cannot "fall" in love just like that real love does not happen by chance it develops over time, the creator has given us the foundation of which to build it on. People do not fall in love, but rather lust. Yet few see the importance of laying a right foundation. Remember miscalculation can lead to disaster. The world does not understand that proper dating and courtship. Form the solid foundation that a relationship need to stand on.

So most relationships are built on little more than emotional and psychological sand. When trouble comes failure results because they are improperly anchored. So most are swept away. Because they were never prepared.

See most people will never admit it that they are totally preoccupied throughout their lives with getting, accumulating, satisfying, and focusing on the self. Most view a day with one thing on their mind, most importantly number one person in his life himself. Without God's help one may not consciously admit this. So let's focus if you will on another form of dating the society has made possible. That Internet where you can search to select one or more of many.

CHAPTER 8

The Avenue "To Sex Crimes"

This trend, screams, find you, fool you, forget you. Not only are you selected from the personals/dating category, it can be totally discreet. No one has to know but the two of you.

So let's consider if you will, being available on this website. You not only open yourself up to a broad of people. And most of them are bad, you also have to have your personal business out there for everyone interested to have a look at. Imagine people knowing what it is you are longing for in a relationship. Let alone the devil ears and eyes are wide open. Waiting to attack. Because the mind is the battlefield it's the area where he can attack.

Now here you are, out hear wide open, putting yourself in a position to be attacked. Once again he seek whom he may devour, (the devil).

Statistics show that fast-growing numbers are caught up in

this type of dating, on the Internet. Most feel that the Internet is the answer to their loneliness. Not considering the dangers that lurk. Many, don't even understand what spirits and principalities mean nor are they trying to find out, let alone spiritual warfare. Many may ask, with no sincerity. But yet they are eager to feel out the questionnaire which often include hundreds of different questions. Then after a close analysis your matched. Matched with someone they feel you are compatible with. Let's not forget about the consequences. Will they be a dream come true, or will it be a total nightmare. Remember statistics also show that "sex crimes" have dramatically increased due to this online dating. Needless to say, the danger of meeting strangers through this type of dating, is definitely what you would call a fine you, fool you, forget you move. Setting your self up for the kill.

This remind me of a young lady whom I know and love very much. One day at the tender age of 19 she decided to go online on to one of those dating sites where she did meet a guy, a guy of which she only knew what she read about him. They became what the computer called a match. Question is what kind of match was this? Were there alterative motives all alone? Was this another set up by the devil, to try and break her spirit. It couldn't have been of God. Because God's way is truly different and his content would have changed her life forever. Remember God will guide you, and protect you from endless and usually unseen traps and nasty pitfalls. It's God's intention that everyone of us enjoy a happy marriage at the end.

So anyway, she decided to go ahead and hook up with this guy. Knowing nothing but what she had read, and what he had said. Most, of what she wanted to hear. You see that's how the devil work. They went on and set a date and time. Which no one knew about accept him and her.

Here we are all at the house one night having family fun night. Everyone was laughing, talking, playing cards, just having clean fun. Then of course, here comes the devil, you know he'll have none of that fun stuff if he can help it. He was so smooth, we never knew he had came to pick her up. One minute she was there the next she was gone. Gone off into the night. Some time had passed before anyone even notice she was gone. She just took it upon herself to leave and get in the car with a complete stranger, that no one knew or had seen but her. We couldn't even tell you what color the car was, what color the man was, his plate number or anything, all we knew is that she was gone off, off with a total stranger she met on a computer.

All that was left for us to do was to pray. That is once we were made aware that she was gone. You see we had'nt notice for a while due to the fact we were having family night and people were in and out.

Oh, it finally came to our attention that Missy girl was gone. The phone rang, it was someone letting us know that something had happened. She stated that she received a call from Missy girl and she was hysterical. Screaming and crying in the middle of the street, in the dark. She stated that she had got left there and that she had been raped. Of course, we were all in panic mode. Trying to figure out what happened. Because we know that she was here with us. Just another fine example of how the devil comes to steal, kill, and destroy, and the opportunity was right because of the choice she had made. But thank God for the blood, the blood of Jesus that gives us strength and cover us. Especially in times like these.

All of this, all this coming from just another bad choice. A choice made by someone looking in all the wrong places for what she thought could have turned into love. Not thinking of the consequences she must face. Whether good or bad. And in this case all bad.

So we pulled ourselves together and began to deal with the situation. As the neighbor proceeded to go and pick her up she stopped and called her mother with the details, and made her aware so she could stop and pick her up as well. Why she hadn't called her mom in the first place is beyond me? All I know is once she got there to pick her up, she was still hysterical. There she was in the middle of the street hollering, and screaming with her clothes still intact thank God for that. You see it did'nt take them very long to reach her, so they placed her in the car trying to calm her down as they proceeded to the hospital. She gets in the car kicking and screaming as if she was more angry now than when it actually happened. So it seemed. She continued to act all crazy and angry, kicking the dashboard of the car hollering he raped me, he raped me. I mean don't get me wrong, but like I said it seem as if she was going crazy or something so they say. She kept this up for quite some time. And before you know it her mother slapped her face saying stop it, stop it we will get through this just calm down. There were no other scars present to the eye her mother said so she just needed to calm down and realize that she was safe. Safe from this bad decision she had made. And that it was time to face the consequences.

All who was concerned made it to the hospital, people her mom felt necessary to be there. When her mother's very close friend walked in, she remember seeing her sitting there all discombobulated as if she had lost her mind, because of what happened to her. She remember thinking to herself, the devil is a lie he won't get this one. Remember this was someone very dear to us. She began to pray and rebuke the spirit of depression. You see, she saw what the devil thought he had done he thought he had her mind. But God, would'nt let it be so. As everyone was trying to console her the best way they knew how she began to whisper in her ear the blood, the blood, the wonderful blood of Jesus. She told her to fight and to let it go right now. Told her not to allow the enemy to win. She said to her, he may have took your body, but don't let him have your mind. Told her not to blame or beat herself up. But to just take it in stride as part of the journey and learn from this. She let her know that she had been found, fooled and for gotten, for the moment.

The hospital went ahead with their procedure. The police was called and they told us what we had to do the next day as far as pressing charges, because she wasn't able to respond to their questions at the time.

Okay, a few days had passed. And you see she had never pressed charges yet, she had always been a bit of a drama queen, ever since I can remember. Even as a little tot she always did her own thing, it her choice to wait two or three days before she decided to press charges, so a couple of her friends went to get her and take her to the police station. "Now this just goes to show you how persistent the devil is." He couldn't get her one way, so he showed tried another. Once they got there to pick her up thinking everything was fine. Here she come out of the house dressed like a two dollar hooker. They were dumbfounded they had to do a double take. One blurted out why is she dressed like that? So they proceeded onto the police station anyway. They entered and told the officer in charge that they wanted to report a rape. He looked and asked which one of you would like to make the report, they both pointed to her as she stood there with her miniskirt and fishnet stockings on. Mind you, here to report the rape. So the officer looked her up and down and proceeded to ask her some questions, about what happened. He ask what kind of car was he driving? She didn't know. He ask what they look like? She couldn't remember. He asked if she remember what he even was wearing? She couldn't even answer that. So one may ask, did this really happen? Or was this a sex crime gone wrong?

You see I'm not trying to make this young lady looked bad in any way, my aim is that other teenagers/adults read this story and get something from it. There is most definitely a lesson to be learned here. Remember they hooked up on the Internet where these sites profess to "bring passion and excitement to lonely people's lives, but yet it is being used mainly when looked at as a tool for the devil". Here they are searching one or more of the meaning, claiming to be able to help them find love, at least that's what they call it. For those looking for "a date, sex or a relationship they found the right place". Question is, is this what everybody wants? It's not. Anyone in their right mind realize that this method of dating is dangerous in every way.

Satan has counterfeited virtually every aspect of God's way. Of love and happiness. That's why it is so important "nowadays especially" to be very careful with your heart a date should be an enjoyable activity. The first thing is getting to know each other. Not find me, fool me, and forget me.

With all this being said let's not forget the best way to choose the best person for you is not choose at all, to leave the choice in God's hands. The word says his ways and understanding are infinitely better than ours (I SA. 55; 8). And he is the only one who can lead you to the right person. But we must be willing to do our part.

Remember, God's spirit will not guide you if you are unwilling to wait until the right time to move. It's a process finding and choosing a mate, which is best left to God's overall direction. Allow God to take you by the hand and lead you to that right person, he will if you let him.

CHAPTER 9

What is Really Going on?

Out of all the stories I wrote about in this book I want you to notice first their age and their gender. Yes, you are correct so far they were all women. But I insist that we have an understanding, and both agree, that women are not the only ones who are found, fooled, and forgot. Many men go through the same heartache. You'll be surprised of how many men are raising their kids by their selves or are not allowed to see their kids. How they have been lied to and deceived. Yes they love hard too. This bring to mind about a man I have the pleasure of knowing. He fell in lust or you can say infatuated with a young lady right before graduation. Even though he had already graduated he still had feelings for this young lady who had yet to graduate. "So let the chase begin". Just like a bumblebee, he was jumping from flower to flower, until he landed on this one. She really caught his attention.

See, she was no easy mark. She most definitely gave him a run for the money. He had to date her first. He took her here and there. As time went on they started a courtship. Both young and full of life. They were at least trying to start off on the right foot. At least she was I can say that. Abstinence was the way for her, at least for the first six months. Then of course the flesh began to get weak. Remember pressure will bust a pipe. And when we let go of God's way we make a way for the devil to do his nasty deeds. So we know, how the consequences could go wrong.

Okay, here's a guy one year older, very nice-looking already graduated and has his own car. And he treated her with respect. What more can a young lady ask for. They continued to see each other even though the odds were very much against them at first. Back then she lived in a town that didn't care very much for his town so they rarely saw each other. But they went against the odds and kept seeing each other. As time went on they fell in love so they thought. Remember, they were teenagers mind you. They soon started having sexual intercourse. Which we all know can take a relationship to a whole nother level. Here they are spending more and more time together. So one night he was hanging out with his friends, you know partying and drinking, just hanging out. Next thing he know he told his friend to pull the car over because he was feeling sick. All you can hear is him calling Earl. After it had passed his friend began asking him some questions about him and his girl. His friend told him that his girl may be pregnant. That was just an educated guess. Can you imagine his fear when his friend said that, being a teenager getting ready to have a baby. Even though she hadn't had a chance to tell him, but when he went over there after work the next day her sister answered the door all excited, which made him leary as to what was going on. You see she hadn't had a chance to tell him so he really was just guessing. So he proceeded into the house and he and she sat in their normal area and then she dropped the bomb. He was totally elated to hear that he was getting ready to have his first baby, actually the first grandbaby in the family. He was the oldest of nine children.

He had a job and wanted to do right by her. You see this is the way he was raised by his father and granddad. He wanted to marry her before she got pregnant. But things happen so fast. As time went on they decided to move in together, he still had marriage on his mind. But things really was moving fast that's why once again God's way is always right. We have to put the flesh under submission.

So they went ahead and move together and began to live as a couple. He continued to work "like he was raised to do" and take care of his baby and "girl". Even though it seemed that everywhere they moved their house would get broken into but that past.

Before they had little Junior they went out often and did lots of things together. But things changed. He got a job at Fords. Which was right on time because she had found out that a second baby was on the way. So this job was a blessing for them. Everything was going fine and of course he still wanted to get married even the more. But the job kept him so busy and tired all the time all he could think of was sleep and rest. He needed her to be patient and supportive to what he was going through. She needed to know that he was not neglecting her, he was just dog tired from working. Time went on and she wasn't wanting for anything. So he thought. He was working at Fords 10 to 12 hours per day, not to mention it took an hour and a half to get there. You would think she'd care, no, because self had began to arise, more than ever she started complaining that he wasn't spending enough time with her and the kids and that they weren't going out like they used to. Remember, she was still a teenager just playing house. He tried to make her understand that it was nothing personal. It's just that he was tired all the time, and that he still loved her and the kids. But she just didn't want to hear that. But the devil did and made his move on her.

They continue on with this program and she grew more lonely. I guess you can say, he kept on doing what he felt was right, but he started filling unease when he came home, something just wasn't right between them. You know when you really love someone you can tell when they change on you. So he decided to do a little investigating. To him things just wasn't adding up. The thrill is gone for one thing. He continued to notice how she would take her phone calls in the other room, stop wanting to have sex, she just wasn't as attentive as she used to be. He even noticed that laughter had gone between them. She had different people calling asking for her, "even though they knew all of each other friends". They were calling for her lover. One day he picked up the extension and heard a man on the other end, as she tried to holler over him letting him know that she was on the phone. But it was too late the gig was up, she was busted. He decided to let it go right then he tried to ignore what was going on and see if things would change between them. Nothing changed much. Then one day she said something stupid to him and pushed him over the edge. As they were having a conversation she was telling lie after lie, and it angered him. To the point where he just exploded. Talk about fine you, fool you, and forget you, she took to a whole another level. She had become a cunning, deceitful person. To a man who loved her wholehearted and would do anything for her.

This man was crushed, here he is doing what he thought was

right and all the time she was just going through the motion. She not only hurt him, we must not forget about the kids. Her first and his. And of course, the grandparents aunts, and uncles. Cheating can be very devastating for many involved. Not only was he forced, "after trying to hold on" to let her go, he lost out on seeing his kids grow up. Even though this was not his heart's desire. He wanted nothing else but to raise his family. But all her devious ways left him no other choice but to walk away. The man could take no more. She used the kids as a pawn during their breakup. By not letting him see them. Adding more fuel to the fire.

You see this pain is not just for women, it goes both ways this man have been betrayed in every way. But I can'nt help to think, that, if he would have went ahead and married her, would their relationship have turned out better? That's if they would have done it God's way in the first place, could all this have been avoided? If abstinence would have stayed in play? Soon as they started fornicating, "whether they realize it or not" they had displeased God as many of us do, yes it's true, he done right by her, so he thought. He was not doing right by God, because he never married her. They continued to be led by the lust of the flesh. That's why Paul wrote walk in the spirit then you won't for fill the lust of the flesh. Which are contrary one to the other: so that you cannot do the things that you would (GAL. 5:16 – 17). Which simply describes our everyday battle.

Just another example proving that sex before marriage is never a way, we should choose to test our relationships. Many believe that it is good for it. Nor is it helpful in learning whether a couple is "sexually compatible" before they commit to marriage. This is never the case, as most of us know! God design sex to be a part of our marriage. When it occurs outside marriage, it destroys relationships and ultimately the individuals involved. Leaving us wondering where did I go wrong?

There are numerous teenage couples as well as older couples who sincerely believe that they are in love, after briefly meeting and dating each other. That they would someday marry each other. Looking for a way to validate their feelings, they allow their selves to be guided by their human reasoning. Never really obviously understanding real love. They continue to deceive themselves into believing that they are sharing and giving. That they were practicing unselfishness. You see they knew they love each other and wanted others to understand. Most are generally incapable of analyzing their motives in a relationship. They either fail, the young lady become pregnant or a disease has resulted. And oh yes virginity is gone and disillusionment has entered. For most, even these events are not enough to jolt them back to reality. Would it be fair to say that most should sincerely analyze the motive behind their relationship and honestly acknowledge the basis of it. While infatuation driven, lust is the driver.

This is why there are so many cases of fine you, fool you and forget you. Notice what our creator God say about our feelings and the heart. He said the heart is deceitful above all things and desperately wicked: who can know it? (Jer. 17:9). He also said the way of fool is right in his own eyes: but he that Harkins (listens) unto counsel is wise (PROV. 12:15). So remember to face the facts.

Vast numbers of people go down the path of sincerely believing that they are in love. Sometimes deceiving themselves into believing this. When actually they are ruining their lives and lives of others. There can only be painful results, from fornication, unwanted children, nasty diseases, disappointments, financial hardship, psychological problems, (some leading to suicide) lost happiness, and futures, this is what happens from the stupid choices we make. Question is, are you walking in the right direction in your dating life? What dangers you might be overlooking? Are they being ignored? Why not set the right priorities, demonstrate character and do the right thing? Guess what, whether you know it or not your entire future could depend on it!

CHAPTER 10

I Have Feelings Too

Remember, God Is Love. He Gave His Only Son to Redeem Humanity. Christ Said, "Greater Love Has No Man Than This, That a Man Lay down His Life for His Friends" (John 15:13). Again we ask what is true love? When we have learned that it is a selfless, sharing, outflowing concern for others which is founded on the way of give. This involves putting one's own feelings and interest aside to better see and serve the needs and feelings of others. Not used and abused and then kicked to the curve. Because God is love, he desires all to have. To experience the same love he has experienced

It is important that we grasp this all important point. True love is unselfish. It is not an emotional high (although it certainly involves emotions). It combine both out going concern and genuine affection for the other person or persons in a relationship.

Remember, it must always continue to extend, to further include other human beings. A relationship must be based on a firm foundation in order to withstand. Being attracted to someone is not enough and would never work. Because God don't bless no mess. God understood from creation that it was* not good that man should be alone". Therefore, he created a wife for the first man Adam (GEN. 2:18) he taught them his law and explained how, if, it will bring wonderful happiness and joy to their lives and yes he'll do the same for us if we'7|ll just allow him too. Most human beings live their lives guided by feelings. Not realizing that absolute destruction lies ahead, if not careful.

You see God's law can be simplified into one word, love. Take a look at the 10 Commandments. They are summarized as love. Love toward God and love to our fellow human beings, one to another. Notice: you shall have no other God before me. You should not make unto you any graven image. Shall not take the name of the Lord your God in vain. And of course, to keep the Sabbath day holy. (EX. 20:3 – 8). The first four teach us how to love God. The last six if you notice instruct man how to love his fellow man.

God's 10 Commandments form the only true foundation of every aspect of the right way to live. This included how to form and maintain proper relationships. They were magnified in the New Testament and are still in effect today. Christ states that "he is the same yesterday, and today, and forever" (HEB. 13:8). Shouldn't our perspectives mirror God's? There are principles that must be applied to be out in a long lasting relationship. During the course of dating everything you do should be based on give. You should continually ask yourself, if your conduct reflects both love toward God and love toward your neighbor? Remember, sin is the opposite of love and yes this does include vanity. And guess what stems from this, competition, strife (arguments), greed, envy, jealousy, hatred and lust. AND MOST RELATIONSHIPS TODAY ARE FILLED WITH THESE ATTITUDES.

The Bible teaches that we have at least one thing in common. It states "for all I have sinned, and come short of the glory of God" (ROM. 3:23) that's every man, woman and child who has ever lived. So therefore, Sin is the breaking of God's commandments. Of course, none of us intend on sinning, we just fall short, like the Bible say. Because even when we obey the letter of the law, we still break the spirit of the law in our mind, and this also is sin. Sin begins in the mind. Because given enough time what you think about eventually becomes what you do (PROV. 23:7). So your intentions may not be to fine, fool or forget a person. But, by you not being aware of the right procedures it take for a relationship to last, you'll find yourself in this position every time you choose to do things your way. Most never make the connection between thoughts and actions. James 1:14 – 15 demonstrates that wrong thaughts eventually produce wrong actions.

This reminds me of when I was a younger adult and a friend of mine was in lust with this young lady who lived over in what we call the whole. He had been seeing her for quite some time off and on because he was on the rebound and had just got out a relationship, in fact that's part of the reason he fell for her so quickly. But for some reason I never thought she was for the right things being so young and reckless. Don't get me wrong I grew fond of her, in fact you could say I became close to her. You see he as time went on, he had been through some things with this girl, things that brought them closer. You see she had a little baby boy when they got together, just an infant. Her son died during their relationship from S.I.D.S the poor baby was found dead in bed. By this time my friend and his whole family was loving on them. He was calling the baby son, yeah it was that serious. So, of course, he was there to help her through her ordeal. Time went on and they were still a couple they thought they were so in love they began to talk about marriage. Yes marriage. Remember what I said about relationships being built on feelings. Here the feelings included sympathy.

Yeah, I even began to look at her different. As time went on, they came to a place where they needed a place to live. And of course, my friend invited her to come and live with him, thinking this could be a test run before he married her. You know how we do. So she took him up on his offer and they moved in together. So here they are living happily ever after so they thought. And of course things seem to be going well, and you know who had to come and stick his nose in it, Mr. Satan himself, sending one of his best demons for this task. Remember on which their foundation was built on, feelings and emotions. As I was saying everything seemed to be going fine between them better than I would think, due to the fact he hadn't been too long getting out a relationship with a girl that I know he loved very much. My friend was ready to pop the question. He had got a good job and everything. He was ready so he thought to take the big step. Even though he would never admit that he was vunerable at the time.

You see my friend house was full of life and excitement. We would all gather down there for hours on playing cards or what have you. Just enjoying life. You see we were raised to be giving an outgoing. We wouldn't dare turn our back on someone in need of our help. Months had gone by since the tragedy of the baby. But that don't mean another one wasn't on the way. One day while they lay asleep the phone rang. It was his cousin in need of somewhere to stay. This was one of his first cousins mind you. He's only about

4 to 5 years younger than him. So of course, my friend being who he is told him to come over, it'll be alright. So here he come back to bed all with a smile on his face. Don't forget he also had the woman there to, and a new job. Now I don't know about you. But this sound like nothing but trouble to me. I started having concerns for friend, but you couldn't tell him anything right then his head was still in the clouds. Life was good for him at the time, until trouble came knocking.

This man thought he had found his suitable lifelong mate. But I knew that was a lie. Their relationship was not built on a solid foundation. It was just an emotional love as with anything of value, emotional maturity takes time and effort to acquire. It never stood a chance, especially when his cousin got there. And not to mention his ex-started popping up unannounced. Not only that everyone was telling lies on her saying that she was cheating on him even though she wasn't at the time. I've always said that his cousin was sent by Satan personally. I remember he always thought he was God's gift to life he thought he had the magic touch when it came to women. Apparently he had something (his cousin).

Time went on and things seems to be going well at their house, although it seemed. He continued working leaving them in his house while he was gone. His cousin had no job mind you. He put his trust in her as his woman, that's why he didn't have any concern about her cheating. Even though this is what he was hearing on every turn. She was real cool with her stuff, until she heard that he had got the other woman knocked up. At least that's the lie she was telling, to get him back. Oh yeah, you know how the devil do. He really drops the bomb with his consequences. But love is blind. She wasn't happy about the news. Remember they had just buried her baby son. This brought her heart nothing but pain.

Once again, I found myself all in because of the love I have for my friend, although I still had my concerns. I decided to give her the benefit of the doubt. Not only that he started to change on her every since he found out about his ex being pregnant. He tried to argue and fight about everything. He became very mean to her that was proof he steel had love for his ex-. One day she just showed up uninvited. So of course the young lady would act out on him. He immediately took his ex-side and started accusing her of cheating. He continued to push her away for the ex, but she tried to fight for him, but he just wasn't listening. Before I knew it, her and the ex got into a fight. And everyone seemed against her. She found herself all alone and that's when it happened she turned to his cousin for comfort, he would see the way my friend had treated her so bad and he began to offer her his shoulder to cry on. She was just a young girl and had no one to turn to she tried to tell him that the baby the ex was having, was not his. He continued to treat her harsh, he would go to work leaving her in tears. So of course being human she started accepting the comfort from his cousin. As time went on they became intimate. He made her feel like there was hope. He didn't like the way my friend had treated her, even though that wasn't an excuse for their actions. Most people think that sex is the answer to ease their pain. But believe me, it only leads to destruction. Especially when you have to sneak. You're just asking for trouble.

Remember she said that the other girls baby was not his, and she was right, it wasn't. But guess what, turns out she found out that she was pregnant also. Torn between two lovers due to the circumstances she had my friend think it was his. After all she was still suppose to be his girl, before all the craziness that was going on. Even though she felt as if she was sleeping with the enemy at times, she still had love for him. Even though he believed his ex-. Thing is, he had never let go his ex-, that was the problem from the beginning. They should have never been together. That's what I mean about those feelings. He had been played like a fool by his ex-. Seem as though he was trying to play her as well. But he'll soon find out who was the fool.

Time passed on and along comes this beautiful little girl. Later that night I get a phone call. She said I would like you to help me name my baby girl. Of course, that made me feel really good. Not knowing it was the works of the devil and his games, I went ahead and helped her name the baby. We came up with a beautiful name. A name no one else had. To this day I never heard that name again. So here they come home with their bundle of joy. Thinking they would live happily ever after. Unfortunately, not so, he was blindsided. As time went on the baby became sick. And like they say what goes on in the dark will come to the light. He was so busy thinking like a dad he still didn't come home from work, he rushed to the hospital anxious to find out what was wrong. The baby was in need of some blood. So of course my friend being the babies dad so he thought at the time, (remember he was just a young man steel blinded by lust and full of emotions) rush in to volunteer his blood. So they began to prep him for the transfusion, And as you know they had to check his blood type against the baby's before they could do anything. A few minutes passed and the doctor came rushing into the room and told them that the baby would be OK. All he could feel was relief, giving God thanks for the baby's life. They continue to live together along with his cousin who hadn't left for the Army yet, like he had planned. They kept on living the life that they had become to believe was right. My friend still working and doing what was right in his heart as a man. He had came back to earth. He continued to take care of her and the baby. And his cousin went off to the Army. All while he was in the Army he knew in his heart that the baby could be his. She had become of age when he came home. But all the while he was gone he was sending her money, clothes etc, because he knew in his heart it was true, they knew what they had done. Not intending to hurt anyone, just the consequences of their sinful choices. Choices made from being hurt. Eventually, after paying child support for the child my friend discovered that the little girl wasn't his and he had been paying for a while. Guess that's the price he paid. But it didn't stop him from loving her they stayed friends and they all forgave each other, because they knew it was all there fought, this is what you call a triple header all four of them was found, fooled, and forgotten. But thank God they knew what forgiveness is.

Just remember, love is the same! think about it. It cannot happen overnight or in an instant, take your time and just allow God to hook you up. This scenario taught us that you may feel that physical attraction immediately, but real, deep love is entirely different be careful with your heart, and literally "take heed lest you fall" (1 I cor. 10:12) and lust, not love. Don't allow your human nature to deceive you. Many have been blinded, to their own hurt. Will this be you? Remember love develops only through careful and proper dating and courtship. A relationship can be a wonderful ordained institution by God. If you allow it to grow and develop. Very few are taught that they must learn to control their emotions. They have been programmed to act accordingly to their feelings, no longer basing decisions and actions on solid moral values. Times have changed dramatically since this ordeal. This was a brief look back at the past. It shows that times and morals have undergone a drastic change. Nowadays people don't know the meaning of a date. Back then sex was shameful out of marriage, making fornication and his tragic results much less frequent which simply mean this situation was rare. And it just goes to show you, that most people then also did not know how to select the right mate either.

CHAPTER 11

What's Your Level of Maturity?

Different levels of immaturity are best described as an epidemic afflicting millions today. What is your maturity level? Assuming you are of sufficient age. Are you certain that you are growing in maturity? Can you probably handle dating and possibly courtship, which will eventually lead to marriage? So therefore, real maturity is absolutely essential to successful dating. Most people do not find it pleasing to date and immature person. If you are immature and refuse to grow, and can't find yourself able to develop and emotional and mental maturity and stability, then the only people you will be able to date, will be the same, immature and unstable people. Those who are stuck and keep getting the same results. More important, before becoming serious and you become older and begin dating one on one, you should have already achieved a certain maturity level. One which will allow you to maintain a serious relationship. A marriage and commitment may be just over the horizon.

A person must mature enough to understand the process of a serious relationship. At least the formalities. We must come to a place in our life where we realize that things don't always go our way. Many young people and adults battle moodiness, often pouty, and becoming easily annoyed when the attention is not on them. Therefore, seemingly every "issue" or crisis causes them to go to pieces. Now how mature is that? This is exactly why so many appear mature but in reality they are terribly immature in every way. Worse, and even more, most individuals now refuse to take responsibility for their action. Somebody else always made them do it. Nothing is ever there fault, always the victim. This is called the blame game.

Again, take heed! Analyze where in your personality and character, you need to grow and develop. Let's work on these areas first set goals and move forward. Ask God to show you other areas in which you need to grow. Ask yourself these questions. Can you make right decisions? Do you take responsibility? Can you handle setbacks? Can you cope with crisis or do you fly off the handle? Do you acknowledge your faults? Do you know the difference between infatuation and real love? Are you patient with others? Are you usually happy rarely allowing things to get you down? Do you feel like you are in control of your emotions? Are you generally thought of as a responsible person? We need to address these areas in our lives in order to maintain a healthy relationship.

Not only is maturity crucial to every aspect of adulthood, it's a vital building block for dating, courting and ultimately marriage.

One must be spiritually, emotionally, and intellectually mature! There are no exceptions. While most same physically and mentally able to enter a relationship, but are often unable to maintain one. Relationships are full of twist and turns and many lack the qualities necessary to endure the ups and downs they'll experience during a relationship.

This is why many of us get caught up. Not planning to be found, fooled, and forgotten. Just settling for the immature and unstable ones. Thinking we can change them, when change comes from within. Maturity is directly related to responsibility. Yet sadly many of us as young people, and believe it or not some adults, never take time to plan their future. Instead one night of lustful impulse can bring disaster crashing down on foolish unsuspecting mind. Because most like to live for the moment, not thinking of the consequences it'll bring with it. Like an unwanted pregnancy, forcing couples to begin preparing for a family without the joy of planning. That's why it is important that we be willing to shed society's influence over us. To learn almost everything we have absorbed over the days of our lives, and replace all this foolishness with sound biblical principles. Once armed with this new set of values, we can firmly rely on God to bless us and guide us to the best possible mate. God's way will reap far greater rewards than you can imagine.

CHAPTER 12

We Can Wait

There was once a time when women dressed more modestly, they covered themselves more. Even the men dressed different. Just like dressing, ways of dating has changed, if that's what you want to call it nowadays. If a young man wanted to date a young woman, he would first ask her father for permission, and at some point ask if he could court her. "Well", we all know that ship has sailed. This is because people generally had more character than those of the modern age.

Young couples use to be chaperoned on a date. That vanished quick. But even yet, young people still understood limits. They may have shared a short kiss, but only after their interest was serious or they were engaged. Unlike today, things are totally different for couples now. Society flaunts sex in everything today, where "fooling around", "making out", "necking" or "heavy groping" and sexual relations are considered the norm. Long before couples consider, let alone entertain the thought of a lifelong commitment, couples nowadays have no restraints. They go straight to permissiveness.

Dating "if that's what you call it" is now a practice that in most cases, almost immediately involves sexual intimacy. Most today disdain or haven't even heard of the concept of courting. Teenage morality, WOW, has dropped to it's lowest point, with no apparent end insight except they find Jesus, and learn to understand the God ordained purpose for sex. Let's not forget the many ways of being exposed to such activity. Television, the Internet, music, billboards, are all ways of feeding them the wrong message. So many may not make the shift fast enough.

Even though times has changed, people tend to forget that there are always consequences for their actions, whether young or old. Really and truly girls just need to keep their skirts down and the panties up. Not make it so easy for the bumblebees (boys) to pollinate them. To stand with integrity. Realize that they are worth more than rubies. Don't allow yourself to become one of their sperm banks, if you get what I mean. Insist on your respect. Don't become a doormat, allowing people to just wipe their feet on you. Remember you are one of God's greatest creations. So are you boys. You could restrain yourself if you choose to, then you won't be trying to put so much pressure on the young ladies. It's called abstinence, give it a try I guarantee you'll live.

CHAPTER 13

Shouldn't We Date First

First of all teenage dating should only be within groups and with specific parental knowledge and permission. One-on-one dates may begin as one grows older, and closer to the age suitable for marriage. But let's face it, things are far from this. It's gotten to a point where they don't even listen until it's too late. And even then it goes through one ear and out the other. Half of them don't even know what a date is, let alone courtship, which is sad. This is why, you see, so many babies having babies, and not a father insight. Because they didn't want to take the time to date and get to know the other person. At least through group dating you have a chance to overcome nervousness and learn to relax and naturally respond to those of the opposite sex, avoiding that pressure. This will allow you to evaluate situations more realistically. Above all, try to date widely. This simply mean for one to date as many different people as possible that's man and woman. This gives one exposure to a broad range of personalities, with the important side benefit of learning which kind of personalities are compatible with yours and which are not. I'm not saying have sex with these people, not at all. Just get to know them first before you even think about giving your body to them.

Whether you realize it or not, this is most critical to recognize. It's important that you know which kind of people make you comfortable, and which do not. More than likely you will find that one personality type that makes you most comfortable. But this may not always be the case. Not only do you learn about yourself, you are also helping your date to do the same. Dating widely helps you interact with almost anyone, any kind of social setting. Romances never to be involved, in the earliest stages of dating. This is where many of them go wrong. They think if they get romantic with the person in which they are dating it all make the relationship more complete. But they are sadly mistaking, sex only complicate things. And teenagers are much too young for this serious, yes serious activity. Recognize that society is pushing you from every direction to begin romance long before it is appropriate. Romance to early carries a high price. Many have had to pay this price and have had to get through the storm, they had to rebuild their shattered lives. Thousands of teenagers have grown up to sorely regret the daily pain and consequences they now face, because they thought they were more mature, more ready for romance than they thought they were. And when I say group dating, I don't mean pairing off.

I'm simply talking about a group of 6 to 8 or so just enjoying a wholesome activity together. Parents must be particularly watchful of less responsible teenagers, there the ones who think they are the most responsible. Those who think they can handle it long before they are in fact ready. Yeah, I know a little about that. One must remind their self that dating is the first step of the process to find the mate with whom you plan to spend the rest of your physical life. But before all this, you must be converted.

Let it be understood that a responsible adult or parent should stay close during all this group dating. Age 18 is the absolute soonest that a person should consider dating one on one with 19 to 20 a better age to start this activity. However, whatever the age this begins, which is sometimes too soon, it is vital to have already laid a foundation. One of exposure of all kinds of settings of those of the opposite sex. There should be a certain comfort level before one on one dating even began. Otherwise, the danger grows. The more shy, timid, or nervous a person the sooner they'll pair off with either the first person with whom they find comfort or whosoever pay him or her attention. And as a parent you often find yourself living this nightmare, if you don't encourage your child to group date. This is a way, For them to overcome nervousness and learn to relax and naturally respond to those of the opposite sex. It will also be beneficial when moving on to the more serious step of courting. Especially if they end up dating someone with more experience than them. More experience does not make you a better mate for someone.

This is why it is critical to discuss the dangers of "going steady" now more referred to as "going out". Society has accepted this trend and yet it is wrong and produces much untold misery. Many find themselves in these so-called long-term relationships and tend to just fall forward into this next seemingly natural step. Ready for it or not it will eventually lead to marriage. It is clear that the purpose of dating is to find the right person to marry! God will provide that special person when the time is right. But, once again, only by waiting for God selection and timing. Remember to continue to date widely in the meantime. You'll know when you've found the best possible person.

Ever notice so many begin to go steady through high school, and some on and into and through college. Not knowing with certainty if they have found the right person. Even though they think it's right. But because the immaturity that most have, and because they are not allowing God to guide them, they just can't be certain. Question to ask is why do teenagers go steady? Often due to peer pressure, and changes within themselves. Lots of teenagers are extremely insecure. And they go steady for many reasons. One of the main reason is to gain a sense of security. Some use it as the easy way out of wondering or worrying who will take, or will ask them to go, maybe to the movies, a school dance, party, or sports event, or just out to eat. This is a way of having a built in date for all social occasions, this also is a great way of being part of the "in crowd". Then there are those who go steady because of their lower level of emotional maturity. This is a easier way than asking for dates, conversing, and inter acting with someone new. It enables teens to cover up shyness and bashfulness. Once going steady you can relax more, not worry about putting your best foot forward or even trying to impress the other person. Even though dating should never be solely about impressing the other person anyway, we'll keep that as the first meeting. You have to wonder if the ones who do go steady as teenagers, ever stop to ask, "if I haven't dated widely, how can I possibly know if I love this person I chose to go steady with"? If we fit together? And yet foolishly so many with no experience really believe they are "in love". Not only does going steady eliminates the opportunity for social development amongst others, it is the lazy, selfish, short sided way of avoiding rejection, shortsighted and dangerous method of dating. It seem to mean premarital sex when you really look at it. When basically what they are doing is merely stealing from the happiness of their future marriage. Including, stealing from their future mate. Just from acting on this selfish sexual desires.

Even though boys may never admit it, they know that going steady over a long period of time makes it much easier to convince the girl to give in to that fleshy desire "sex". Once again pressure will burst a pipe. Not only that, some will go through all that, just to get the panties. And once that has been accomplished they are ready to move on. Leaving behind yet another broken spirit. The emotional distress of a breakup. It is important to always demonstrate the necessary willpower to make the right choice now instead of choosing "to enjoy the pleasures of sin for a season" (HEB. 11:25).

There are other serious potential side effects of going steady for a long time. Even without fornication. Not only can you find yourself fooled and forgotten. You spend all your time with that person, canceling out dating others. There's a great chance you will inevitably later compare your future spouse to him or her. Because you tie yourself to that person. Not saying that this is always a bad thing, it all depends on who's guiding you. You know what they say that early dating leads to early marriage, which leads to early divorces! So you see a lifelong pattern can develop from what seemed so harmless in the teen year.

So if you are tied in a "steady" relationship, you probably feel your situation is different. Yeah, you probably think that you love each other. Yet, if this were true, you would immediately break it off. You wouldn't wait until you were both able to properly develop the relationship and, more importantly, until God shows you that he is gotten in it. Which will be done on his timetable not yours! Remember, dating was meant for people to get to know each other. It is the perfect means to develop the ability to communicate well with others. It will benefit you in countless ways of life. Not only will there be old friendships, open doors, and help you succeed in the world later. Communicating and tactfully expressing yourself take time, but dating widely helps to teach you these things. Dating can help to build your social skills and grace. It will also serve as an opportunity to grow intellectually. Unfortunately, among those who are younger, this is absent today. Dates should be uplifting and at least interesting. Rarely do you see to young people and most young adults actually sitting across from another holding an interesting, let alone fascinating conversation. What you mostly see is to people browsing their phones and looking down, not having eye to eye contact. So how can they find their selves interesting to each other? This is the time to share wholesome ideas. Ask questions about each other. Discuss interests. Both parties should strive to be active and interested in making the date a learning experience.

Is important to learn to express your thoughts with color and enthusiasm, and try to expand your vocabulary by learning and using words while on your date. Trust me you'll find that others can find you interesting, and even fascinating to talk to. Believe me, you will stand out to those who think and enjoy a good conversation. And don't forget it is important that you strive to become an attentive and active listener give your date and others a chance to express themselves as well. A wise man once said, "big minds talk about ideas, average minds talk about things, and little minds talk about people". Which of these describes you? An important goal in every date is to have a good time, and to let your light shine.

CHAPTER 14

Learn from Each Other and Grow

One thing I've learned over the years is that it is important to learn something from each other while being involved in a relationship. One thing is for sure, dating different people help to develop your personality and character. This is why for the life of me I can't understand why so many women continue to have all these babies by multiple men. One would think after you have been found, fooled, and forgotten that first time, one would learn from their mistake and grow from it. Take a whole new approach, like God's way for instance. At least this way will guide you and detour you around those pits of heartbreaks.

Let's face it, there is nothing funny about raising 3 to 4 kids all by yourself. When you know in your heart you expected that man to be a man and be there like he said he would. You'll be surprised, just how immature people really are. I mean, who am I to judge, that's not my intention, I'm just sick of seeing all the heartache and pain we cause each other. Especially when I know it can be avoided, just by doing it God's way.

You see dating should be an enjoyable activity for all involved, not a set up to deceive each other. And yes, an important goal in every date is to have a good time. Do not neglect to plan your date. Trust me, it's very important that you do. Something specific should always be planned. I can't stress it enough how important dating is. We can most definitely cut out a lot of these unwanted heartbreaks, we allow ourselves to endure. Remember, there are more places to go other than the show. Which virtually assault the senses and have no real worth of value. Remember this is just a door to getting acquainted with each other. So be sure to be relaxed and try to enjoy yourself and get to know the opposite sex.

Let's not forget that dating helps to develop your personality. Date widely, with a variety of people, you not only get to know different personalities but you also learn to understand them. You will observe aspects of their personalities and you will learn to deal with certain Indiosyncrasies (foolishness) in people. Even though you may not want to date a particular person, you will still benefit from a wide exposure of people, and you may want to emulate from some. Learn to be comfortable around the opposite sex, take charge sometime observe aspects of their personalities. It's okay to throw yourself into unfamiliar situations and plan dates that will force you to converse. Every man has something to offer everyone and vice versa. So go ahead and give it a try.

Unfortunately, society today seems to be in a continual "battle of the sexes". Both sexes are led to believe that they cannot truly figure each other out. This is false and it makes it too easy for both sexes to say "you don't understand me at all." Evolution might, God would definitely not! Just because experts and psychologists may not be able to understand because they ignore God's instruction manual. You can. Be careful don't assume too much in this area. Set out to understand the opposite sex. You'll benefit from it. Understanding the difference between men and women will be of utmost value when you do marry. Learn to recognize and genuinely enjoy the many other differences between men and women. Just be careful not to stereotype. It's important that a man understand a woman, how else would they successfully lead a woman for life, and help her achieve her greatness. And trust me a woman simply must understand her man so that she can inspire him to be the best he can be. Just think without properly understanding each other roles how can they work towards growth, benefit and success?

While there are obvious differences between men and women, lack of communication and understanding one another is vital for a relationship to last. It's sad when outward appearance is the sole determining factor when it comes to choosing a date for people. More often the average looking man or woman have a better personalities, more character mixed with vanity. Basically because they have not been as inclined to spend all their time focused on themselves and good looks. So what you'll get is the real thing.

Dating, a wide variety of people does give you some advantage. Not only does it help build your personality, it helps you to make better choices when it come to settling down with just one person. A good personality involves a positive outlook on life. It includes a genuine interests for others and attentiveness to them. It also include a good sense of humor, enthusiasm and adaptability. One will possess a good personality is versatile, flexible, and able to interact with a variety of people and a wide range of interests. Things that are needed for healthy relationship to maintain.

One thing is for sure, going steady does not develop one's personality. Because when it end to early a wonderful opportunity is lost. This is why I say having a steady boyfriend or girlfriend puts a person into a comfort zone that restricts the vital ongoing development of personality. Your personality should be vibrant alive and interesting to the point others would find it fascinating to be around you. When you pair off to early its hardly conductive to your personality. Again that's why as you date more widely, certain personalities will appeal to you. Certain attributes will be more or less attractive to you. When you date try to be kind, gentle and considerate. These are traits that can always be improved. And when you date you will learn. In the end dating is a tremendous opportunity to exchange, grow and improve, your personality. Also is at least in part a character building activity as well.

The Bible teaches that love "does not be have it self unseemly" (1 cor. 13:5) why not try to make it your goal to "esteem others better than yourself" (PHIL. 2:3), giving to others, making them feel special. In dating, little things mean a lot. Just like other aspects of life it take practice. Strive to be a gentleman or a lady. You will benefit in the end.

CHAPTER 15

God's Way or Else

A lot of us don't even want to face the fact that this is Satan's world, he does not want mankind living God's way. Do you honestly think we enjoy being found, fooled, and forgotten. Of course not, he wants confusion of rules in every possible way. A sexless being, he wants man nor woman to know their worth. Sadly, there is a wide spread of male abuse of women, and equality that has come at a terrible price. Most do not realize that there are God design God ordained purposes for men and women.

It is important now more than ever, that each man and woman know their roles. Are women striving to be feminine in the way God intended? or do they accept the pressures and influences of society? And man, are you truly masculine in the way you were designed to be, or are you guided by the thinking of a confused world. True masculinity has been undermined at every turn for quite a while. That's why there's so much pain when trying to maintain a relationship nowadays. Men are depicted as morally weak, unintelligent and lacking the character to make any decisions, let alone the right ones when it comes to family. I'm not talking about all men of course, there are some good men with their head in the right place. Men, who realize their role and know that they are the head and not the tail. But I am talking of those immature fellows. You know, the ones who act like a bumbling fool much too often. It's important that a real man take the lead, the way God intended. Why? Why should you continue to be an ineffective leader who have to be "bailed out" of problems by screwed, sometimes conniving, sharp tongue, more competent women who think they know everything. Making yourself look weak, barely functioning. Stop being identified as one who only survive through the continual assistance of an intelligent assertive women. On the other hand,

Women don't want to be pictured as aggressive, and more masculine than their counterparts. Strength and courage are rare in men today, with most having become weak and indecisive. Sad but true. Taken their anger out on the women, failing to take their leadership roles, leaving women to feel the void. And you ask why dating is so important? At least you know what you're getting, most are disconnected to God. Reverse roles cause unhappiness, unnecessary tension and severe frustration in a relationship which only leads to more heartache.

God created man first and put him as the head, the leader over the woman in the marriage relationship. But those even mostly fulfilling this God ordained role have all but disappeared. "Oh Lord please bring our men back to reality". Yes it is true, that man was created physically different from women (Proverbs 20:29) describes how the glory of young men is their strength. He was designed to be the provider. On the other hand, (1 Peter 3:7) describes women as the physically "weaker vessel" to whom man must "give honor". Don't get me wrong I know how these women are today. Far from what the Bible say we are "meek and quiet spirit".

The difference between men and women are not just physical. Their mental and emotional levels are as well. So you see there are many reasons why so many are being found, fooled, and forgotten. Because relationships are not starting off on the right foot. Once again a lot of this pain can be avoided if we always strive to do things God's way.

Don't misunderstand me, it's a great feeling to be on "cloud nine" to be in love. Few things in life are comparable to this filling. Nevertheless, sound judgment can still be made, without heavy emotional attachment. Think of this if you will this way: it is important to pay attention to those who set the right example, but also learn from those who are willing to share their stories of regret and pain. Ask yourself, if you will, "am I going to learn by following a right example, or will I force myself to learn the hard way, by following my will instead of God's will"? I suggest that you pay special attention to those who set the right example. Remember in this world dating and courtship are built on lust most of the time. (1 John 2:16) says "for all (all means all) that is in the world, the lust of the flesh, and the lust of the eyes, and the pride of life, is not of the father, but is of the world".

One thing for sure, for love is of God; and everyone that love is born of God, and knows God. It's good to remember the kind of "love" in the world is always selfish. And that a carnal person is not capable of having anything but selfish love. So good luck to those who think they'll find that perfect mate, there is no such thing.

They are no perfect people, including you. So good luck looking for that 100%, they don't exist. We all fall short.

It is of the most importance that you be connected to God whenever you begin your search for love. (Amos 3:3) ask, can two walk together except they be agreed? The answer is a big fat no! God states plainly, be ye not unequally yoked together with unbelievers; for what fellowship has righteousness with unrighteousness? And (11 Corin. 6:14) ask, what communion has light with darkness? This passage here offers no exceptions to the rule. So I suggest you think before you move.

Remember it's important to be mindful and avoid every circumstance that involves extensive fellowship with those of different beliefs from yours. This will cut out, the uneven yoke being together, or even married to an unbeliever. Really and truly, one who has God's spirit and has been baptized and converted is prohibited from dating one who does not. So this is something you may want to take to heart, you don't want to get with the wrong crowd, if you get my drift. Even though it may seem itself, the wrong crowd has become the only crowd, keep the faith, God is still in control. Therefore be extremely cautious if you do choose to occasionally step out on a date with those of different beliefs. They will influence you. And something else to remember, your mind is already naturally (whether you believe it or not) hostile against God (ROM. 8:7). Even though they may not set out to purposely influence you, it will happen with time. So you may want to take caution.

It's important to know that real Christianity is lived 24 hours a day, seven days a week, every minute of an hour. So you might want to grasp this all important point when choosing your next date. If the person in whom you are interested in does not believe the full truth of God as you do, you are in disagreement from the beginning with him or her, and you still cannot walk together. So this is just a reality you'll have to make yourself come to grip with.

Please do not dismiss religion as merely something that can be worked out after you're married. This is something that should never be compromised. Don't just act as though this is just a minor detail in your life. You will be making a grievous mistake. This mocks God and his way. Yes you'll be married but God won't be involved. God sees through all such charades. And you bets believe your marriage won't be blessed. Why take the chance.

Simply saying if the date has went further and moved on to courtship stage without both parties becoming spirit led (ROM. 8:9, 14), break it off completely until both are converted. It's a great way to avoid the pain of being found, fooled, and totally forgotten.

Recall that the world is all about "falling in love at first sight". No! This does not happen! Most of us continually look for a quick fix in life. Not understanding that doing things God's way almost always take time! And remember, that sex is designed by God to be the "glue" that binds husbands and wives. If you allow your mate to become the most important thing in your life, you have put God into second place, and you don't want to do that. If you always make sure that God is first in your life, all other areas benefit. You can believe that your relationship will experience more growth and truly be the best it can be.

AMEN
MATURE WOMEN

Printed in the United States
By Bookmasters